www.finishinglinepress.com

Last Call

poems by

Nathan A. Kozach

Finishing Line Press
Georgetown, Kentucky

Last Call

Publisher: Leah Maines
Editor: Christen Kincaid
Cover Art and Design: Nick McNeish

Printed in the USA on acid-free paper.
Order online: www.finishinglinepress.com
            also available on amazon.com

                    Author inquiries and mail orders:
                        Finishing Line Press
                          P. O. Box 1626
                      Georgetown, Kentucky 40324
                            U. S. A.

Table of Contents

11:00pm

What Happens When You Write In a Jiffy Lube Waiting Room

There is a desperate moment
when you've waited so long
that even the vast expanse
of an iPhone's unlimited
capabilities can no longer
hold your attention, so you
finally look up at the fellow
inmates, trapped in the same
Waiting Room Hell, helpless
to the racket of ratchets
and the din of drills, firmly
grasped by hands attached
to smelly teenagers who can't
possibly know the difference
between a Volvo and a Ford.

Pen in hand, you notice
the man sitting to the right
is nauseating, the musky
scent of body odor mixed
with tobacco, you wonder
how it is possible he hasn't
died yet. Add in the paunch
and this man's a ticking time
bomb that could keel over
at any minute, sickening everyone
in the area like a human nuke
filled with tar and bacon grease.

The woman across the room
can't afford to send her kids
to daycare, for all three clamor
for her attention like pixie-stick
fueled salesmen, exhausting mom
and exasperating the rest of us.
Can't blame the kids though,

you'd be bouncing off walls
too if you were that age, stuck
in a room, waiting for something
to happen, being too little
to understand what the heck
you're doing there in the first place.

But then the kid trips over
your foot and starts to cry,
and the mom casts a face
of disapproval in your direction
and you notice the fat smoker
sitting next to you can see
everything you are writing,
his face contorted in what
can only be an angry scowl,
so you decide you might
be better suited outside,
a solid brick wall separating
you from those you offended.

Some people just don't
appreciate art these days.

The Lunatic Rantings of an Enraged Starbucks Customer

"Well, they've done it now
Christmas may as well be cancelled.
After all this time, all the progress
we've made as a country,
you wouldn't think bigots exist
and yet we have a corporation
Hell-bent on tying Jesus Christ
to the Rockefeller Christmas Tree
and lighting the damn thing on fire.
Remember when the season
was all about reindeer, roasted
chestnuts and frozen snowflakes?
Where the hell is it now? Gone,
that's where. nothing in their place
but a two-tone red cup, meant
to 'embrace the simplicity and quietness
of the holidays.' Yeah, okay.
More like embrace the profitability
of atheism, if you ask me.
You just can't trust anyone anymore,
not even the goddamn coffee shop.
This isn't the end, let me tell you.
First they give Ol' Saint Nick the boot
next they'll have signs on the doors
saying 'Christians, Keep Out'
with a big red X over a picture
of Jesus. Then they'll be hosting
Bible burning parties, 'You bring
the kindling, we'll bring the coffee.'
Goddamn. The whole world's gone
to Hell. Is it too much to ask my server
hands me my order with a polite
'Merry Christmas'? What the hell
is this 'Happy Holidays' bullshit?

Goddamn America. It's so full
of insensitive jerks these days."

I looked over at the counter line
To see the voice that was so bold
In speaking like this in a coffee shop.
I eyed the shabby man with tired eyes
And posture that screamed defeat
As if the world had given up on him.
Feeling the holiday spirit, I walked
Over to the man, shook his hand,
And told him I'd pay for his drink.
"Thank you, boy. It's nice to see
Some Christmas spirit still exists
In the world." I'll never forget
The look on his face once I leaned
In close and whispered, for only
Him to hear, "Happy Hanukkah."

Quick Sip

You ever notice that humans always
make a mess of everything?

The Bethlehem Gas Station That Refused Mary a Bathroom

Squirming uncomfortably
alone in leather seats, empty
bottles littering the vehicle
(driving is thirsty work)
My search for refuge
from the pressure built
up like an obese man sat
upon an air-filled balloon.

The Sunoco sign greeted
me with welcoming arms,
The arrowed logo pointing
as if to tell me my journey
had come to an end, follow
the North Star home my child,
Amen and Hallelujah.

Past the aisles of Funyuns
and Fritos, KitKats and
TicTacs, The door appears
as if out of a dream, nirvana
is here, the faded, dusty sign
shining in my eyes as if it said
"Treasure, dig here", instead
of the more likely "restroom".
But Old Man Jerkface growls
from behind his perch at the counter,
"Public not allowed", as if I planned
on stealing his toilet for sale
on the black market, or perhaps
I was expected to set the damn
thing on fire and burn the place
to the ground, laughing maniacally.

That restroom may be heaven,
but relief came to me in hell:
I bought gum with a fifty dollar
bill, and asked for change in ones.

20 Reasons Why I Think I Get Why Garfield Hates Mondays

The weekend's over.
It's always raining.
There was no hot water
in the shower.
I cut my face shaving.
I'm out of milk.
A car splashed me
on the sidewalk
during my morning
walk to work.
The pen in my front
pocket exploded.
I have to go to a meeting.
I get yelled at for being
wet and inky.
I forgot my lunch.
I got emailed my credit
card bill. (can't afford it)
I have to slosh back home,
praying another car
won't soak me.
 I have nobody to greet
me at my door.
I burn my hand while
making tea.
I STILL have no milk.
The cable is out.
I have no good books.
My neighbors jam
to death metal
at all hours of the day.
It's not Tuesday.
It's STILL not Tuesday.

12:00am

My Girlfriend is Having an Open Affair

When they are together,
happy, a puppy salivating
at the dish, pure, primal, unbridled,
ecstasy and adrenaline fueling
a PB&J perfect match for each other.

Their meetings are public, coffee
shops and restaurants, my presence
penetrating their romantic bubble,
their consistent PDA is intimate, voyeuristic
romance porn, open mouths, desirous
gazes, mixed with some tasteful tongues.

She likes me too, of course, her smile
says it all, her koala squeeze a reminder
she's staying by my side, one hand
locked securely in mine, the other
python-grips the solid shaft of her
spoon, her fork, the vessel
to her one true love.

An Apology to a Preachy Alcoholic Vegan Who Told Me I'm Poisoning My Body

I'm sorry I eat bacon, burgers,
and turkey. I'll stew in remorse
as the tryptophan
settling in my satisfied stomach
nudges my eyelids
downward,
the shades of a window
drawn as I drift to guiltless sleep.
I'm sorry milk is "disgusting",
the same magic liquid that you
claim is toxic calcifies my bones
(have you ever broken one? Not me)
I'm sorry you prattle on about pigs,
cows; We agree they might not be
treated well but I think the name
"Cowschwitz" is in poor taste, maybe
I should refer to your garden
as Buchenwald,
you caused the great
carrot genocide of just last week.

I'm sorry you think your healthy, as you
slowly die much quicker than me.

I Am No Longer King of My Castle, Now That I Have a Queen

It starts off pleasant enough,
late-night walks hand in hand,
early-morning cuddles, eyes
barely open, each smiling face
indicative of mutual contentment.

But suddenly, clothes are strewn
across the floor, as if my hamper
contained dynamite as well as clothes.
Vegetarian sausages sit patiently
in my fridge, doesn't the woman
know the real thing tastes better?

My Netflix queue has been filled
with shows I've never watched,
as if some hacker a hundred miles
away is scarfing stolen popcorn
and enjoying Grey's Anatomy,
sponsored by My Bank Account.

Different, yes, irksome, of course,
but for some reason it is all okay,
her intrusive presence integrated
into daily routines, like an air freshener,
it stings the nose at first, the olfactory
organ gradually enjoying the smell of lilac.

Am I better off with her? The smile
on my face tells the whole story.

Quick Sip #2

Funny how we only feel frustrated
when people don't do what we want.

Being Overly Ambitious with a New Notebook

With these   blank pages
I will write words evoking
emotions, lofty vocabulary
hiding my authorial intents,
clues amidst the consonance
waiting to be discovered.
With these   blank pages
I will create works of art,
my pen as a paintbrush,
the language my watercolors,
subtle pastel sadness mixed
with overbearing vibrant wit.
With these   blank pages
I will provide commentary
on the world through my
eyes, with biting sarcasm
I'll tackle hot button topics
and controversial concepts.
With these   blank pages
I will scribble out mistakes,
misspelled words, stanzas
plagued with poor rhythm,
entire pieces thrown away
never to be looked at again.
With these   blank pages
I will doodle aimlessly,
cubes and stick figures
littering the wordless pages
hiding amongst poorly drawn
trees and dilapidated houses.

I can dream all I want, and
tell myself I'll be ambitious
with these   blank pages,
but nothing good lasts
and the only words in the book
are eggs,
apples,
 milk.

1:00am

A Box of Childhood Photographs That Scared the Hell Out of Me

Something about the box
Always made me feel nervous
As if it would suck me in
Like a black hole if I ever
Got close enough to fall
Into it, trapped in the paisley
Cardboard walls until the rapture
Comes and burns the contents
Of the box to microscopic dust.
But sometimes I would venture
A little too close to the edge
And get a glimpse of whatever
The box might contain within.

There was a boy at the bottom
No more than two, in a polka dot
Birthday hat, grinning from ear
To ear, showing teeth that had not
Yet seen the wonders of oral surgery.
He was holding in his hand some
Type of truck; the look on his face
Satisfied, as if that one toy is all
He needed to be happy forever,
Trapped in an endless moment
Of pure childhood bliss.

The boy frightens me, ensures
I never peruse the other contents
Of the box. I know his smile hides
A deep sadness, one that starts within
And slowly works its way outward,
Like being sucked out by a vacuum.
His despair will overcome him, slowly

But surely, as he gets older he'll feel
The weight of life become heavier
And heavier, he'll see the boy
With the happy smile and know
It'll never last, because nothing
Lasts forever, and happiness
Is nothing but an old photograph.

Getting Super Emotional About Tetris and Life

It always happens the same way:
you're stuck, waiting
for the perfect moment
for everything to move
into place, for all your work
to lead to immense success,
the finish line of a marathon;
a precarious line of dominoes

You see it clearly, exactly
what you need to complete
your goal, your heart beats rapid
as it inches towards you,
cementing your victory
as everything slides into place.

And then it is all gone.
 Everything disappears, like water
on a hot sidewalk, never
to be seen again, evaporated.
What was the waiting for?
What did you accomplish?

Quick Sip #3

I can't decide if I am more afraid
of the past or the future.

You Won't Care if You Can't Care

Floating through an endless vacuum
Like a jellyfish in the open ocean,
Not a care in the world. Nothing
Can trouble the mind when the mind
Isn't there. No reason to love
When there is no heart, no purpose
In laughing when one cannot laugh.
The tides shift around me, but I
Can't feel them, can't care my life
Is being thrust in a direction
I have no control over, to a place
That could be better or worse,
Makes no difference to me, not
When I can't worry about what's
Coming around the next corner.

Can a creature survive in such
A state of apathetic melancholy?
Works for the jellyfish,
It'll have to work for me.

Last Call

It's such a misused phrase, pal.
It doesn't mean an end,
despite what you may think.
It is actually an opportunity,
a chance to change your mind.

It's "Speak now or forever hold
your peace", the moment right
before you kiss her for the last
first time, the moment when
all doubts slip away like the veil
partially covering her smiling face.

It's the last offer on your new castle,
the first place you finally call home,
together, the chance to create
a life worth living, a place to stare
into her eyes as she drifts to sleep
each night, both of you wondering how
you got so lucky to be in that moment.

It's the final warning you give your
child, an opportunity for her to
get it right, to show you she's learned
a thing or two about the hot stove,
a chance for you to show her you
love her, your arms a gentle barrier,
protecting her from the world.

It's a chance to get on that boat,
that plane, take a journey, make
friends, snap a picture for your
"Stuff I Did" album. It's the final
moment before you jump
from the bridge, supported
by a thin cord, adrenaline fueling
you like no coffee ever could.

Sure bud, it's a well known
fact: every "last call" is the
beginning of opportunity.
It's also the beginning of regret,
but that's a story for another time.

www.ingramcontent.com/pod-product-compliance
Lightning Source LLC
LaVergne TN
LVHW021124080426
835510LV00021B/3309